BRAIN GAMES™

OPTICAL ILLUSIONS

Lower Your Brain Age in Minutes a Day

Publications International, Ltd.

Cover Image: Shutterstock

Interior Art: Edward H. Adelson, Alamy Images, Archimedes' Lab™, Art Resource, Corbis, Dreamstime, The Grabarchuk Family, Robin Humer, Jupiterimages, Gianni Sarcone, Shutterstock, SuperStock, Jen Torche, Herman J. Verwaal

Contributing Language Consultant: Elizabeth Barker is a copy-editor and proofreader based in Thame, Oxfordshire, England. She is experienced in localising books from American English to British English, copy-editing Microsoft Word and PowerPoint documents for publication, correction of academic texts to the relevant standards for publication and creating puzzles and crosswords.

Brain Games™ is a trademark of Publications International, Ltd.

ISBN-13: 978-1-4508-4688-2
ISBN-10: 1-4508-4688-2

Manufactured in China.

8 7 6 5 4 3 2 1

Contents

Seeing Is Deceiving!

For all the complex and fascinating things neuroscientists have discovered about the human brain, it still remains the most mysterious part of our bodies. One thing we do know is that the brain's interpretation of the world isn't always literal. When it comes to perception, our brain is good at filling in gaps and drawing visual conclusions that may not align with reality. These are more than just psychological tricks and ocular illusions—in an effort to keep our surroundings familiar and understandable, the brain takes a few liberties here and there. And for the most part, none of us ever notice what we're missing.

In short, we often see what we want to see.

It's no wonder that optical illusions are so fascinating. They have, after all, been around for centuries and have been utilized for a number of purposes: psychological exams, creative advertisements, and just plain fun! Over the years, they've also been employed as educational tools. In order to decipher a typical illusion, your brain is functioning in ways it isn't accustomed to. Stepping outside of your comfort zone and thinking in ways that are creative and challenging to your visual perception is exactly the kind of exercise the brain needs. Consider it a trip to the cerebral gym!

You see, scientists have shown that working puzzles can increase your brain's flexibility, or neuroplasticity, helping to fend off the mental decline that often happens as people age. Just as going to the gym keeps you physically fit, completing puzzles—here in the form of optical illusions—keeps you mentally fit. Our brain functions like the muscles in our body: The more you use it (i.e., work out), the stronger it becomes.

So don't be mistaken about the illusions found in this book—they do much more than play with how we see the world. These are intentional manipulations of space, depth, colour, and shape. They are designed to get your cognitive motors in gear, your perception heightened, and your concentration razor sharp. And, most importantly, they're a lot of fun! Your brain will be boggled and befuddled, but before you know it, you'll be a champion of spotting and deciphering illusions.

The illusions packed in this book are as diverse and richly designed as they come. You'll find:

- Ebbinghaus Illusions, which deal with size perception
- Müller-Lyer Illusions, which deal with perceived length
- Ambigrams, which deal with how written language can be interpreted in more than one way

The book is divided into four chapters. The first deals with things that appear one way but may be something else altogether. In the second chapter you'll hone your visual acuity as you search for things that may not be entirely visible at first glance. Chapter 3 dives into illusions involving perspective, and how seeing sometimes isn't believing. And, finally, in chapter 4, you'll journey through illusions of colour and motion.

When everything is said and done, you may not believe your eyes!

Nothing's as It Seems
Vase or Face?

What do you see here: a vase or 2 faces?

Tricky Terrace

Study both the positioning of the man and the angle of the balcony. Which direction is the man facing?

Answer on page 154.

Crooked Lines?

Not so much. The lines only seem to be crooked due to the opposing directions of the shapes they intersect.

Well-done Illusion

For centuries, artists have manipulated perceived depth within their work, as well as 3-dimensional space. This artist has taken that experimentation a step further, making a public space his canvas. The result? A real shock for the casual passers-by.

Santa Balance

Who seems heavier, Santa or his elf?

Answer on page 154.

Go for a Spin

Check out the circle below; if you stare at it long enough, it will appear to spin, like a record.

The Pulse

It only takes a quick glance to notice something unusual with this picture—namely that the lines appear to be pulsing. This is an illusion of design, created by how the lines change directions within the square shape.

Squares Within Squares Within...

The cube lines fold in on themselves before collapsing at the centre. This is an example of an impossible object, a classic illusion. Impossible objects are defined by their inability to exist in the 3-dimensional world. They look good on paper, but are nothing beyond that.

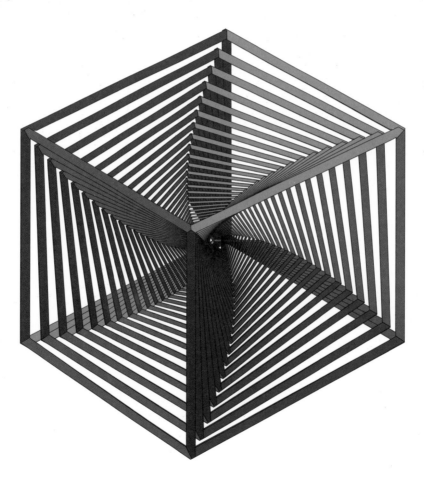

Veggie Face

At first glance, this painting by Giuseppe Arcimboldo appears to be just a random collection of vegetables. Look closer at the precise composition—the veggies form a smiling face.

Scholars

Which of the 3 men depicted in this illustration is the tallest?

Answer on page 154.

Topspin

Move the picture from side to side and make the top twirl!

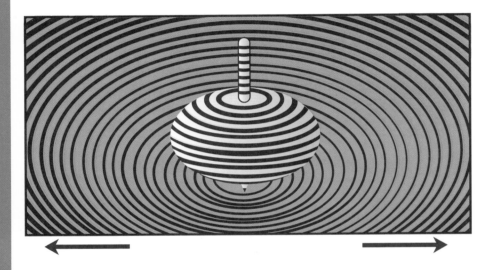

Play It Again...

This is another impossible structure, only here it's a piano doubling as a bar. Kind of gives new meaning to the term "piano bar," wouldn't you say?

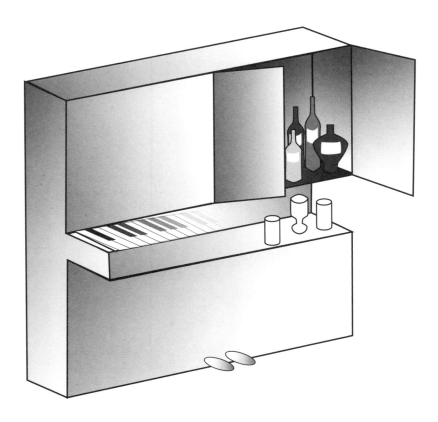

Straight Lines

Stare at this image, and the lines passing through the circles will appear to bend. They are perfectly straight—this is an illusion caused by the rings the lines pass through. The straight lines appear to warp with the curves.

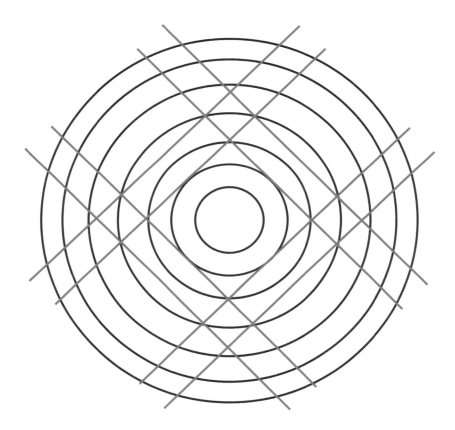

Which Way Is Up?

Are these tiles facing up or down? Also, study the top and bottom rows. The tiles aren't completely outlined; but, because the middle tiles are complete, your mind fills in the gaps.

Chess Set

What do you see here, 2 people leaning in for a close chat or a partial set of chess pieces? The truth is, there is no right answer; it could be either. That's how many illusions work—their appearances are largely shaped by perception.

Cubic

This is a take on the impossible image (though much older, oddly enough). Notice how the arrangement of cubes gives depth to the piece, from top to bottom.

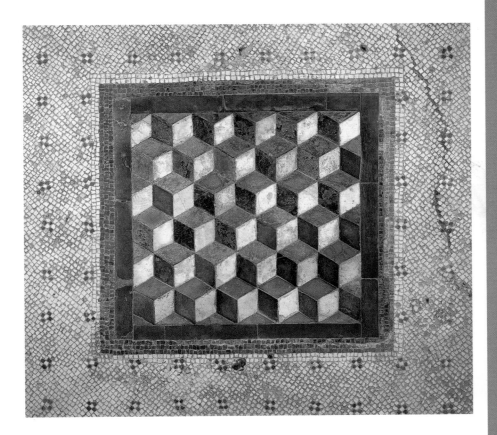

Beware of Illusions!

Humour and optical illusions can be meshed together to create very odd situations. This staircase is an impossible figure that, unfortunately for our passer-by, gave way to a dangerous drop!

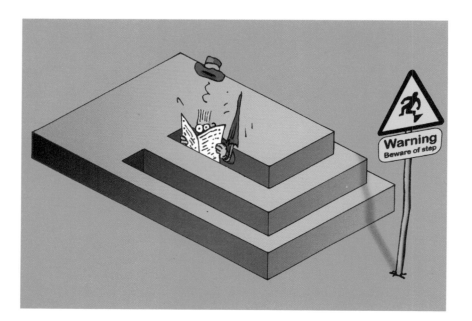

Jagged Lines

Try to follow the black and white lines in this image. Having trouble? The lines aren't continuous—they only appear to be due to a trick of the shapes and colours.

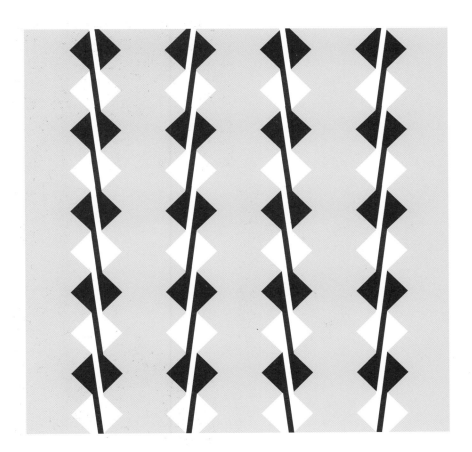

Wine Glass

This illusion involves how we perceive colour. Even though illogical, our mind may lead us to believe that this distortion of colour is a natural reflection, when this isn't the case. It just goes to show how our brain often fills in gaps to create a sense of visual closure.

That's Impossible!

This complex structure cannot exist in the 3-dimensional world. Look at how the joints meet and then branch out—no real figure can have sides that meet and expand in such a way.

Pencil Water

Illusions aren't just tricks of perception and distorted effects. Sometimes, science is involved as well. The pencil below is distorted due to what's known as refraction—a property that causes light to bend. Because of the differences in density between the pencil in the water and the pencil outside the water, light bends it in different ways, causing the warped appearance.

Flower Bed

Like the veggie face seen on page 14, this painting by Giuseppe Arcimboldo is a careful arrangement of a certain element to create an unusual composition. In this case, it's flowers. The end result is a woman's profile.

Curved Square

Look into the centre circle, and you'll see the sides of this square buckle inwards.

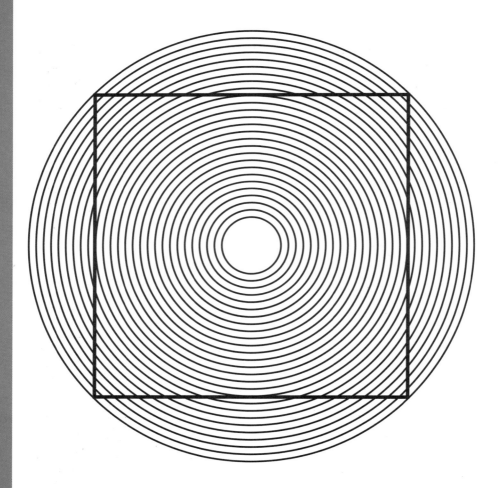

Impossible Triangle

This image, no matter how you look at it, cannot exist in the real world. Not only are all 3 sides perpendicular to each other, there's no way to tell which sides are on the interior and which sides are on the exterior.

CHAPTER 1

Window Frame

This painting from Ferdinand Georg Waldmüller is a fun example of how depth can be creatively manipulated. The addition of the actual frame around the canvas becomes a piece of the artwork itself, creating the effect of looking into a window—and a 3-dimensional plane.

Stacked Perspective

Are these lines straight, or do they run crooked?

Impossible Shape

Here is another shape that, while looking correct at first glance, is actually impossible to create.

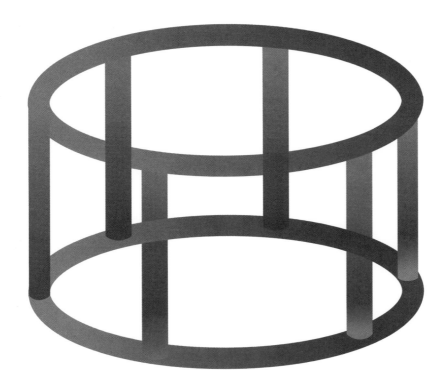

Avant-Garde Illusion

Looks like this is just some creative photography or image manipulation, you say? Think again! You're looking at this blue triangular shape exactly as it appears. It is painted on the building's walls, railings, and ceiling.

Circular Rising

By readjusting some lines in this pattern, it appears that a circle is rising from within.

Spiral Design

Both statues below (**A** and **B**) contain spiral designs. Statue **B** is a mirror image of **A**, yet something is wrong. Can you spot the difference between the 2 statues?

A.   B.

Answer on page 154.

Bull's-eye!

This is another real-world illusion. The yellow bull's-eye is actually painted on the walls, columns, even the TV monitor—if you were standing in this office, this is exactly what you'd see.

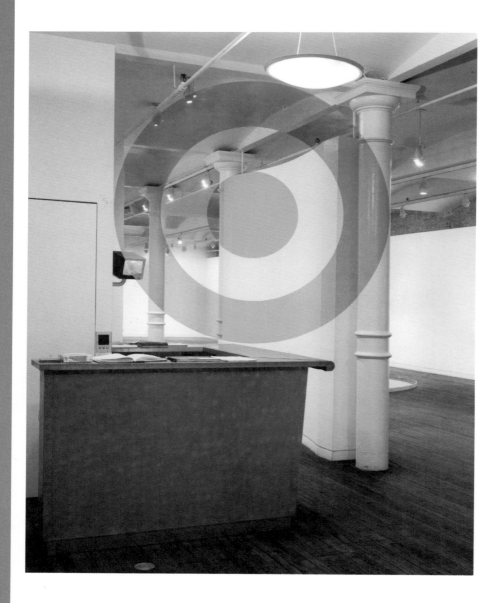

Birdhouse

Begin by looking at this puzzle at normal reading distance. Slowly, move the page closer to your face. As you do, you'll see the bird find his way home.

Summertime Siesta

Here we have another chalk illustration that again plays with how we perceive space. This heart-shaped pool appears to be set within the ground, but it's really an illusion.

Bridge Mouth

By combining a number of familiar objects—trees, a bridge, stairs, houses—a dual effect is created. On one hand, we can discern a man's face; on the other, a town that seems to have jumped from the pages of a fairy tale.

Impossible Fountain

This is another impossible structure, here in the form of a flowing fountain. There's no way the rear columns could be on a separate plane from the front columns.

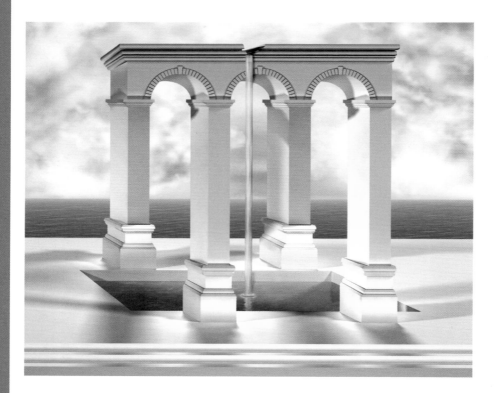

One Small Step

Do you think this footprint is rising out of the sand? Think again. This is actually an imprint, though it appears otherwise.

Funny Bunnies

Something's wrong with the maths here. There are 3 bunnies, but only 3 ears. Yet this image seems on the up-and-up. At closer study, the trick becomes evident—these bunnies are sharing ears.

The Winding Castle

This illustration looks like something out of a fairy tale. The castle's shingled roof and spiral design make it look like a snake.

Lingering Image

We have a task for you: Stare at this skull for 30 seconds. Then, look at a white sheet of paper. What do you see?

Answer on page 154.

Impossible Cube

These cubes stacked on cubes (or within cubes) form an impossible shape. It may look right at a glance, but this design couldn't be created, other than on paper.

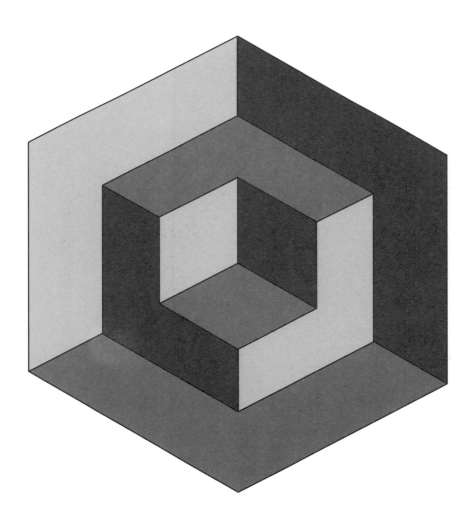

Hidden Within

Eyes Like a Hawk

Ah, the classic illusion of the deceptively hidden object. In this case, though it may seem impossible at first glance, there is a rabbit's head hidden in this hawk. Can you spot it?

Answer on page 154.

Look Closely

What's black and white and hidden in this picture? It's a panda, but you're going to need to find it.

Answer on page 154.

Camel Character

We know this is a camel only by its shape—its actual design is made up of people and an assortment of animals.

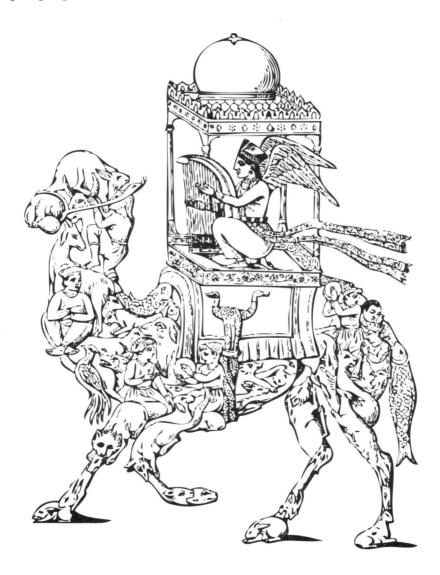

90 Degrees

How many 90-degree angles are hidden in this image?

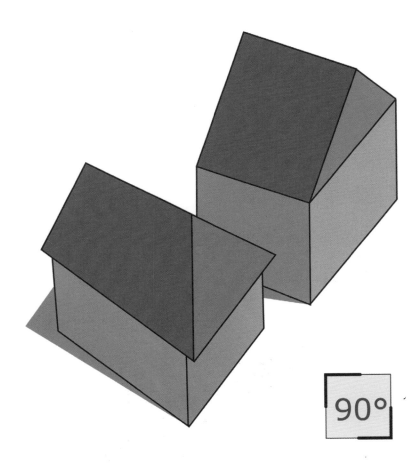

90°

Ahoy, Matey!

Sounds like a silly title, given that this is a picture of a peacock, right? It'll make more sense once you find the hidden image—the face of Blackbeard himself.

Answer on page 155.

Drawing the Line

Believe it or not, but hidden in this line illustration is a cat. Can you pinpoint Kitty's secret location?

Answer on page 155.

Fractured Letter

All the scattered pieces below are fractions of the same letter. What letter is it?

Answer on page 155.

Front/Back

Imagine you are driving and you see the reflection of this car in your rearview mirror. This type of illusion is known as an ambigram. Ambigrams are typographical designs that can be read in different ways, depending on angle, viewpoint, and direction. Can you read the message on the bonnet? What does it say?

Answer on page 155.

Monkey Business

This is clearly a picture of a monkey, wouldn't you agree? But maybe there's something more going on here. If you turn the page upside down, you'll be facing something unexpected.

Author! Author!

This illusion is another example of the subtleties that can be achieved with simple linework, specifically how our mind fills in gaps to create a consistent image. Hidden below is the writer of this evening's production, somewhere very unexpected. You won't see him at first, because he doesn't naturally appear. But once you do spot him, he'll become the focus of the illustration.

CHAPTER 2

Client/Lawyer

This is an illusion dating all the way back to the 18th century. Look at this image as we present it here, and you'll see the face of a lawyer; turn it upside down, and you'll see his panicked client!

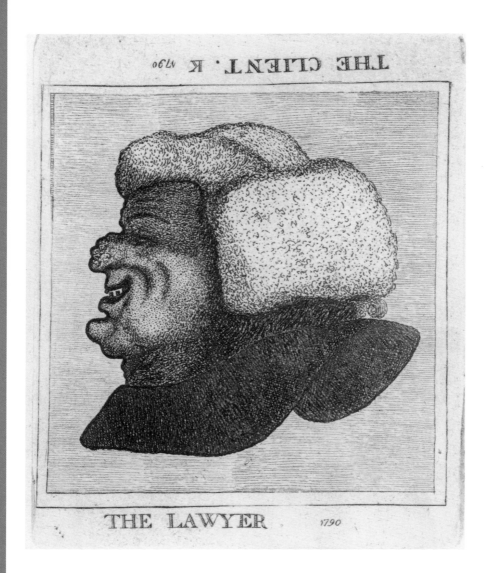

A Comlpete Sentnece

You culod witre a wlhoe sentnece wtih ecah wrod msplseleid jsut as lnog as the frist and last ltteer rieman the smae the hmuan biarn can siltl detremnie waht is bineg wirtetn.

Don't Get Outfoxed

Hidden in this tranquil scene is an outline of a fox. Can you find it?

Answer on page 156.

Here, Kitty...

Here you have the face of a lovable kitten. But look closer, and maybe you'll rotate your perspective all the way around. See the butterfly?

Hidden Woman

Your eyes play tricks on you—it happens all the time. Look at this image below, for example. All it takes is a quick refocusing of your vision, and you get 2 different images. One is of an elderly woman, her face buried in her coat; the other is of a younger woman looking in a distant direction.

Up in Smoke

There's a thief in this man's midst—and he's stolen his best cigars! See if you can focus your visual acuity and spot the cigar thief.

Read Between the Lines

What do you see here: words or black shapes?

THINK

INSIDE

EVERY

SHAPE

LIES

Answer on page 156.

Cheese Vision

Which piece of cheese (**A**, **B**, or **C**) is cut from the semicircle below?

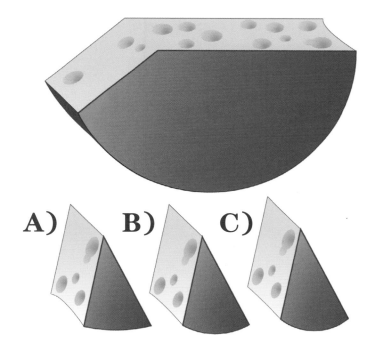

A)   B)   C)

Answer on page 156.

Turn That Smile Upside Down

Like many other illusions, this image gives you one thing while keeping another out of sight. At least sight in the sense of how we're accustomed to looking at things. Turn this page upside down, and you'll turn those grins around as well.

Find the Lovers

Ah, young love. So many times it has to stay hidden. In this case, the clandestine affair is literal. Find the kissing couple in the illustration below.

Answer on page 156.

Ambigrams

Turn the page over: What do you notice?

Answer on page 156.

Missing Fs

How many times does the letter **F** appear in this sentence?

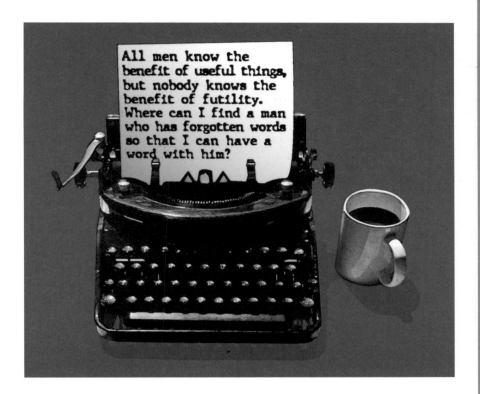

Answer on page 156.

CHAPTER 2

Dog's Best Friend

Can you find the face of this dog's loyal owner?

Answer on page 156.

Baaaffling Illusion

Located in this farmyard scene is the shepherd. Can you find him?

Answer on page 156.

Complete Drawing

Is the drawing below a muscle-bound hulk, or something else? Try to complete the drawing using your sense of humour and imagination.

Answer on page 157.

One of 2 Things

This is a classic illusion where the image can easily be one of 2 things. Here, you have a long-billed duck. But look at it from another perspective, and watch that bill turn into ears, and that duck look more and more like a rabbit.

Impatient Patients

This doctor sure has taken his work home with him. See how many faces of his patients you can spot—we count 5.

Answer on page 157.

Aloha!

There are 2 errors hidden in this hula girl image. Can you spot them both?

Answer on page 157.

Catching Some Zs

Someone isn't finding this Sunday's sermon all that interesting. In fact, it's put him to sleep. Can you find the snoozing figure?

Answer on page 157.

Look at It This Way...

If this horse seems to have a few human characteristics, it's no coincidence. Flip this page over and find out why!

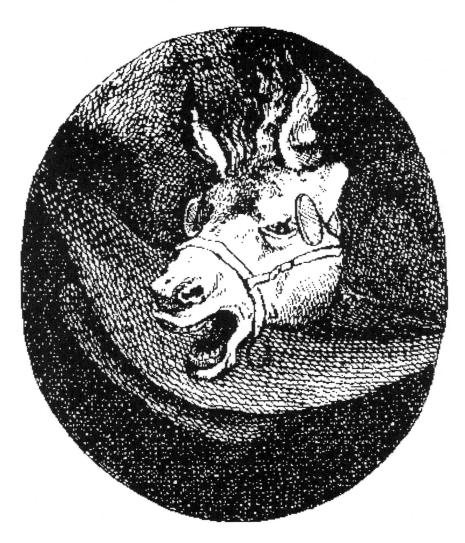

Double Face

Do you see 2 faces, or 3? This kind of illusion, known as an "undecidable image," has been around since ancient times!

Answer on page 157.

Hidden Alien

Can you spot the Martian on this page?

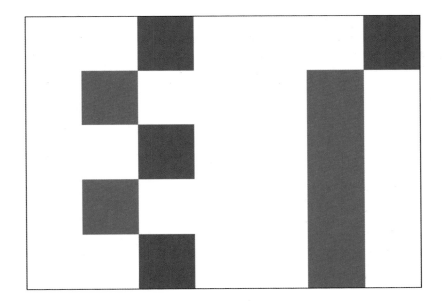

Answer on page 157.

Puzzling Perspectives
Roll the Dice

Study the dice—are the red dots of equal size?

Answer on page 157.

Chopper Lines

Which line is longer, red or blue?

Answer on page 157.

Coy Fishing

Which koi fish is longer?

Answer on page 157.

Bed Lengths

Which of these beds is as long as it is wide?

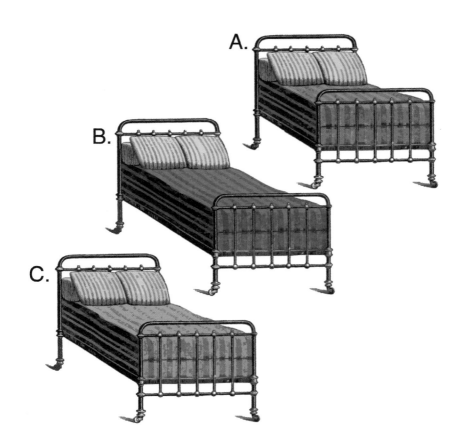

Answer on page 157.

Around in Circles

Which of the 4 lines is the longest?

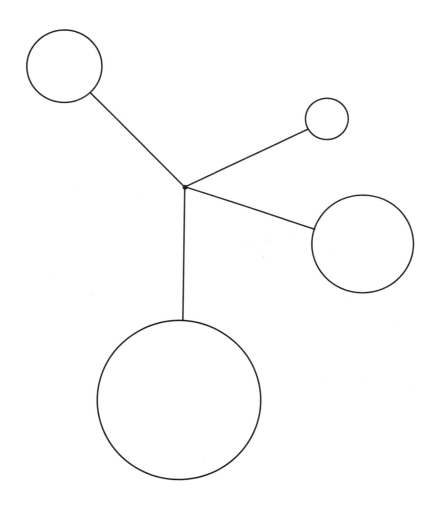

Answer on page 157.

___ Is For...

What letter is depicted here?

N and M

Answer on page 157.

Circular Studies

Which interior circle is larger?

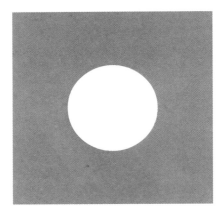

Answer on page 158.

Another Dimension

The box appears to have depth; the circle in the centre of it appears to have shape. But, this is only a manipulation of space and dimension!

Parallelogram

Which line is longer, **A** or **B**?

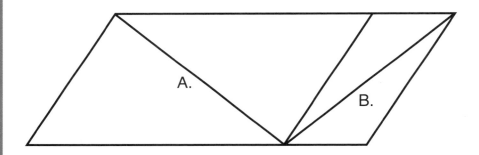

Answer on page 158.

Depth Perception

With creative manipulation of perspective, an image can appear to have 3-dimensional depth.

Pyramid Lines

Are lines **A** and **B** the same length?

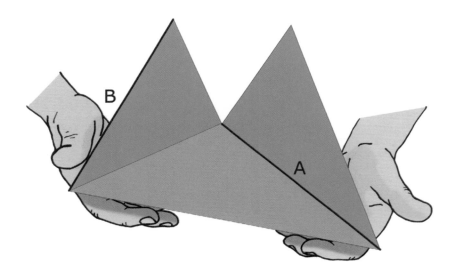

Answer on page 158.

Wall Chairs

It looks like this man is performing an impossible feat of balance and upward movement. The key word here is "impossible." This is just a creative photo—the chairs are actually set on the floor, as is the man.

Wider or Taller?

Is this shirt wider (**A** to **B**) or taller (**C** to **D**)?

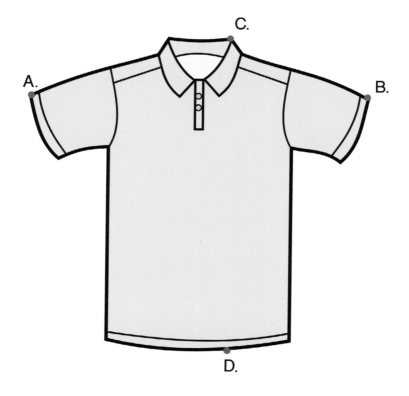

Answer on page 158.

Copyrights

Does each pair of typographical symbols contain letters that are the same size, or are they different?

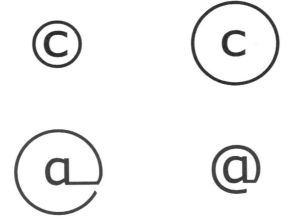

Answer on page 158.

Split Line

Which piece completes the line, the top one or the bottom one?

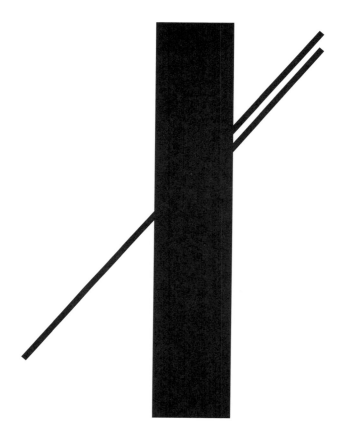

Answer on page 158.

Get Some Perspective

This is what happens when perspective goes awry—this block illustration has no vanishing point, and thus no clear perspective.

Landscape Length

Which line is longer, the red (**A** to **B**) or the blue (**A** to **C**)?

Answer on page 158.

Distorted Squares

Which of these squares is actually a proper, real square: **A** or **B**?

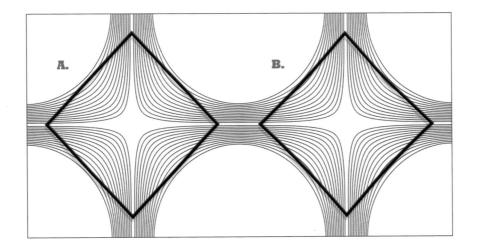

Answer on page 158.

Warping Effect?

Do the horizontal lines warp in the middle, or are they straight?

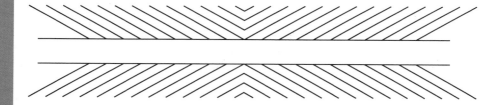

Answer on page 158.

Cube Dots

On which wall does the roaming dot appear? Inner? Outer?
Depending on your perspective, it could be either!

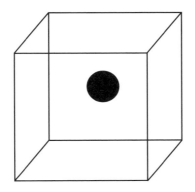

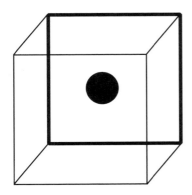

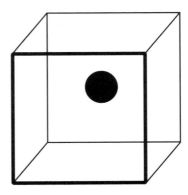

C
H
A
P
T
E
R

3

Time for an Illusion

Can you see the 3 hourglasses? How about the 4 arrows?

Strike!

Which ball is larger, the one in the foreground or the background?

Answer on page 158.

Pick a Number

**C
H
A
P
T
E
R

3**

What number is depicted here?

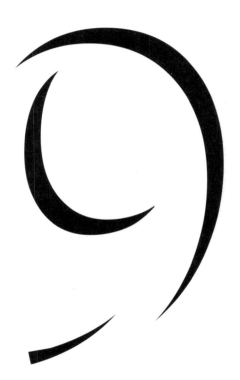

Answer on page 158.

R Shapes

Of the 3 **R**s below, 2 are congruent in shape. Can you find them?

Long Lines

Which line is longer, **A** to **B** or **C** to **D**?

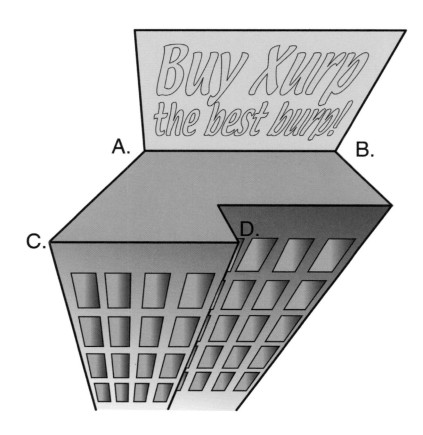

Answer on page 158.

Height Times Width

Which is wider, the **H** or the **W**?

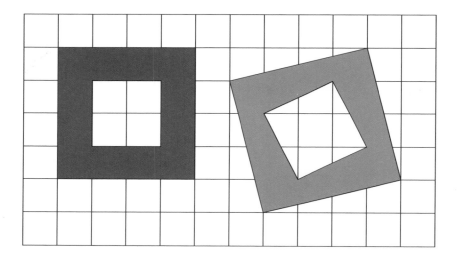

Square Rings

Which ring has the bigger area, red or blue?

Answer on page 158.

Altered Worship

Leave it to Salvador Dali to bend space and perspective in this oddly designed piece. Notice how the inner dome, cubes, and people are arranged: Do you see the makeshift skull?

Warped Grid

With the help of some carefully placed white squares, it appears that a circle is rising from this grid. The reality is that a circular shape is only suggested: Your mind fills in the gaps.

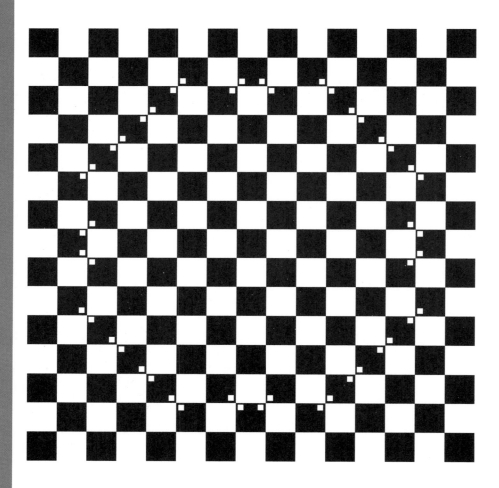

Bookends

Which line, **A** or **B**, is connected to **C**?

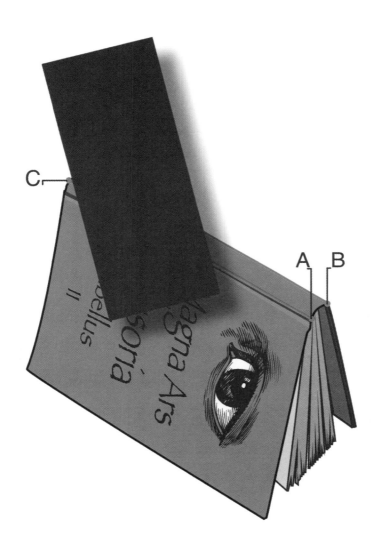

CHAPTER 3

Get to the Point

Nope, this shape isn't coming off the page, it just appears to be. Thanks to perspective and space manipulation, these circles appear to be on the rise—or in retreat, depending on how you look at it!

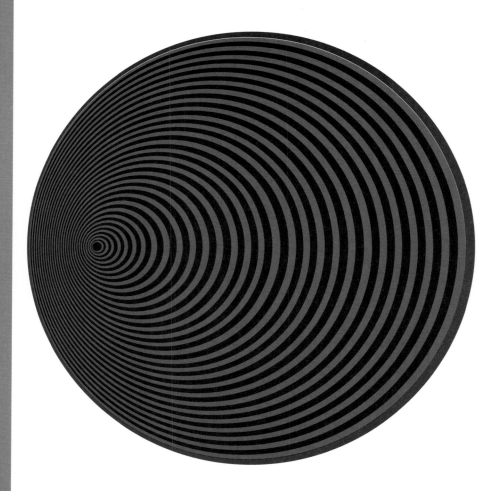

Connected Lines

Which line is longer, **A** or **B**?

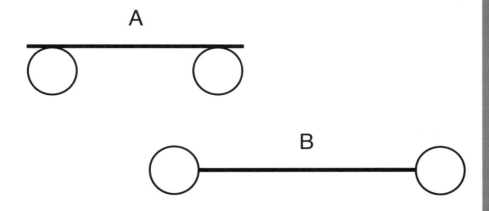

Pick a Number

What number is depicted here?

CHAPTER 3

Answer on page 159.

Totally Cubular!

What do you see here? Cubes? Rectangles? The number 6? The number 9? It could be any or all!

Hands Holding...?

The triangle below is not a triangle at all: The shape you see is an illusion created by the 3 hands and shaded points. The white is the same colour as the background.

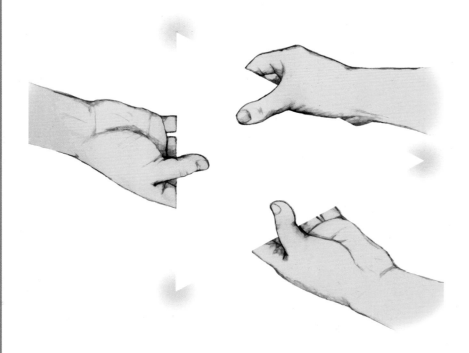

Line Difference

Which line is longer, the one enclosed by the arrows facing in, or the one where the arrows are facing out?

Colours and Motion
Square Holdings

Which 2 interior squares are exactly the same colour?

Answer on page 159.

On a Roll

Seat yourself in front of the image below and watch these ocean waves roll in and out.

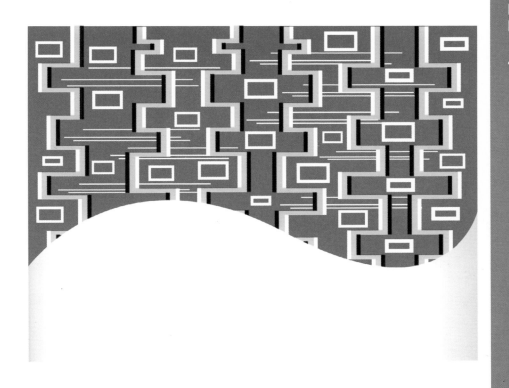

Seeing Things

Stare at this image long enough, and you'll see black dots appear in the white intersections.

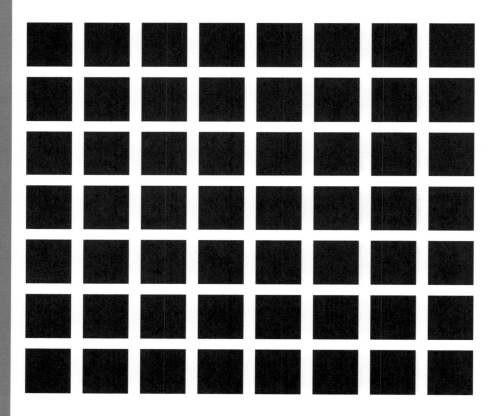

Coloured In?

Although the continents and surrounding water appear to be shaded in (with the colours orange and blue, respectively), they are in fact uniformly white! The colour sensation is caused by the contrasting colour outlines.

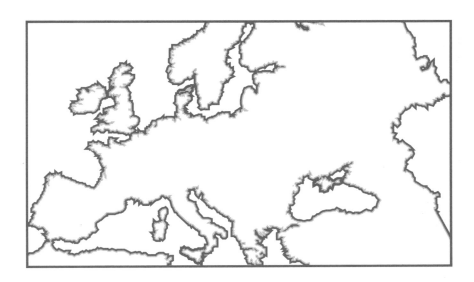

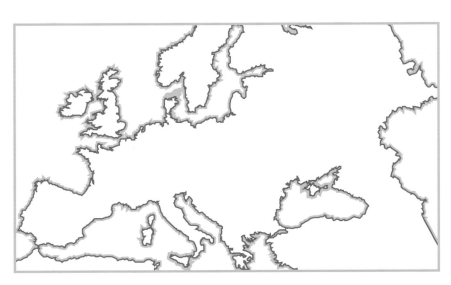

Comforting Illusion

Which colour stripe, **B** or **C**, is an exact match for stripe **A**?

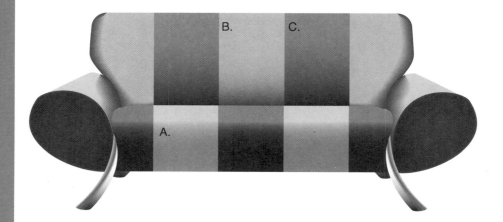

Answer on page 159.

Hypnotic Discs

The overlapping coloured arc segments appear to form spirals, but in reality they are just a series of concentric circles. Moreover, the circles seem to expand.

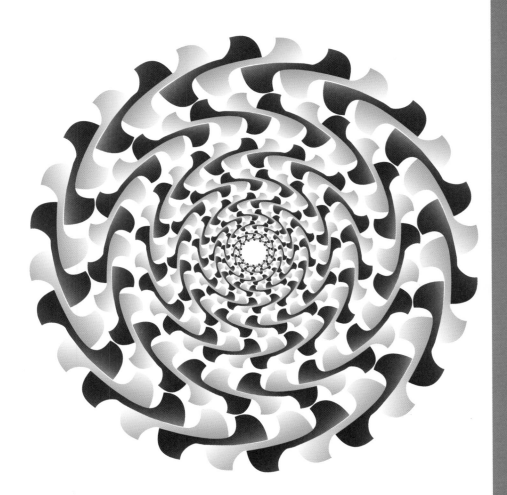

Square Pattern

If you look closely at this image, it appears that 4 lines are running down from the corners of each of the stacked squares. The truth, though, is that all the individual squares are completely uniform—they don't brighten at the corners, even though it appears that they do. This is called a Vasarley Illusion, a sensory effect dealing with light and depth.

Spin Class

Get your bearings as you take a spin through these seemingly moving circles!

Rotating Discs

Which disc rotates faster, the one on the left or the one on the right?

Answer on page 159.

Supernova

Stare closely—but not too closely—at this colour explosion, and watch the colours ripple back and forth.

The Blues

Look at the 2 stars. Are they the same shade of blue?

Answer on page 159.

Shades of Grey

Take a look at this image—it seems like there are multiple shades of grey, right? Actually, there are only 2 shades used. Colours seem darker or lighter depending on the colours they are surrounded by.

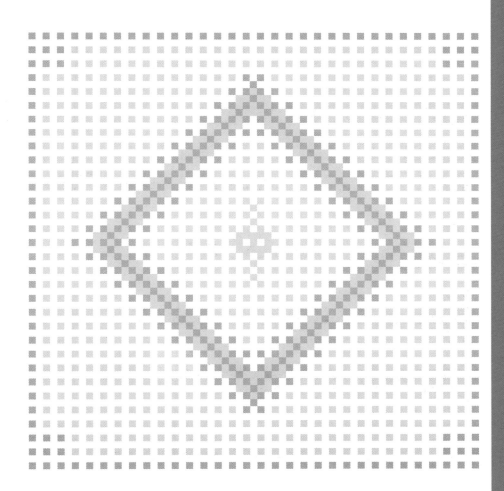

C
H
A
P
T
E
R

4

Bamboo Effect

Notice the shades of grey running within the green bamboos? They actually don't exist! The colour within the bamboos is perfectly even; the illusion of grey is induced by the surrounding grey tones. This is an effect of lateral inhibition, which occurs when 2 contrasting areas compete with one another, causing sensory confusion.

Circular Motion

Move your head back and forth while focusing on these circles. They appear to shift with your movements.

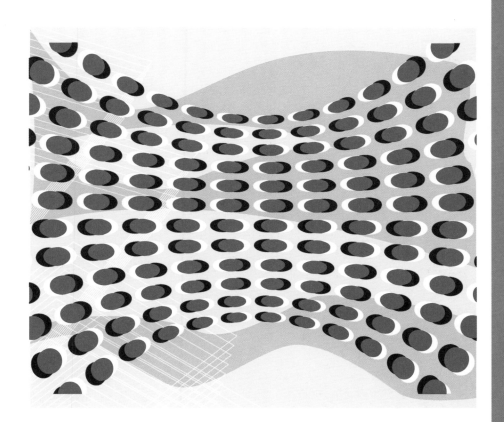

Fade to White

Concentrate on the black circle in the centre. Hold your focus and watch the surrounding grey disappear.

Ghostly Effect

Stare at this image. Notice something? Grey boxes should appear where the white spaces intersect.

Twirling Pinwheels

No, these pinwheels aren't actually moving—though they sure seem like they are!

Shape Jumble

How many different shapes can you spot in this image? There is no right answer; the number depends on your visual interpretation.

Duck Colour

Recover the white colour of this duck's plumage! To restore the colour balance, stare at the **X** in the left diagram for 20 seconds, then shift your gaze over to the duck, specifically to the **O** in the right diagram.

Giddy Up!

Don't be fooled—those spinning discs only give the illusion of movement.

C
H
A
P
T
E
R

4

Winding Abyss

Stare deeply into this image; the circles appear to spiral in towards the middle, even though they remain in straight rows.

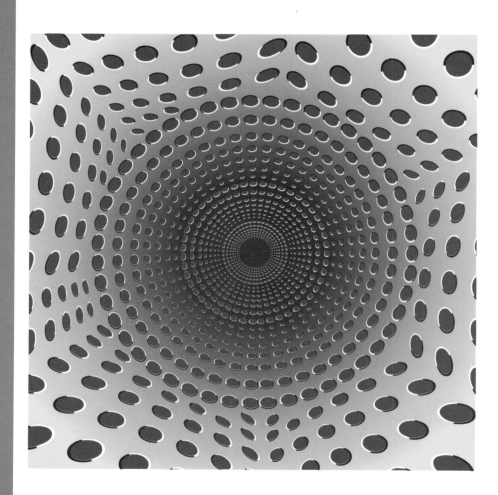

Swollen Illusion

Take a good look at this image—not only does the centre appear to extend outwards, but something else is going on as well. After only a few seconds, grey dots should form where the black lines intersect. This is an after-image effect.

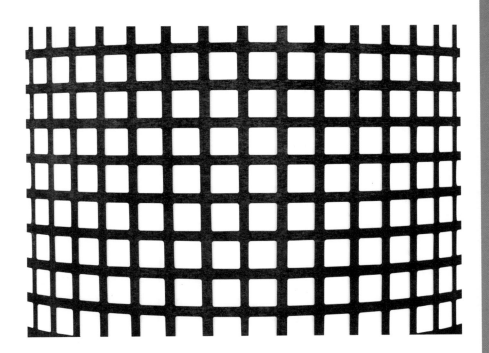

Straw Alignment

At first glance, it seems that all the red lines on the left straw continue into the green and orange lines on the middle and right straws. Is that possible?

Answer on page 159.

Tubes Without End

Focus on the tubes below as they turn and turn and turn!

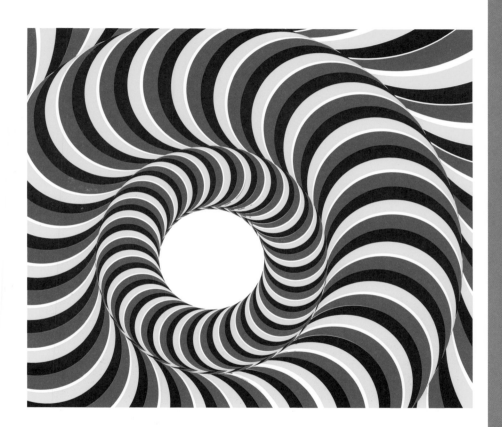

C
H
A
P
T
E
R

4

Crossroads

Are the 4 discs the same shade of grey, or do they vary in brightness?

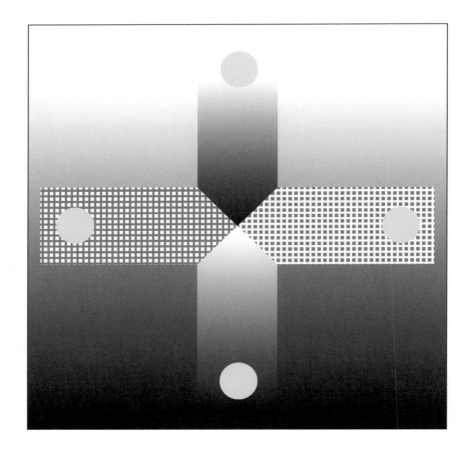

Answer on page 159.

Bar Code

Though these 2 canisters appear to be different shades of grey, they are identical. The black lines crossing with the canister bars on the right make them appear to be lighter.

Spiral Chasing

Stare at these spirals—do they appear to move?

Star Contrast

Are the octagons within the yin-and-yang symbol the same colour?

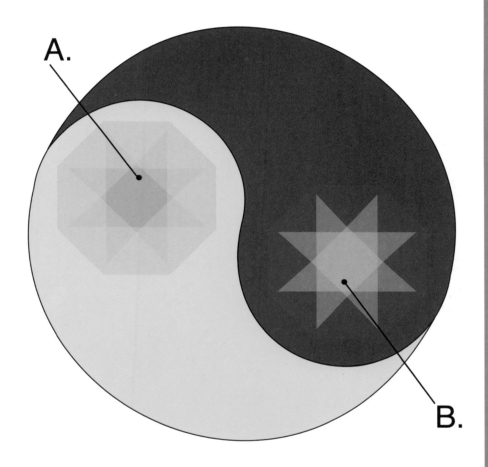

A.

B.

Answer on page 160.

CHAPTER 4

Star Design

Try to focus your concentration on this image without your eyes being diverted to the central points where the lines converge. Difficult, right? The pulsing effect draws your attention away.

Rope Image

Though the middle grey boxes appear to be different shades of grey, it's just an illusion—they are all the same shade.

Colour Explosion!

It looks like these colours are bursting off the page!

Turn, Turn, Turn

Try to keep your perspective while gazing at these twirling circles.

Centre Squares

Which interior square is darker, the one on the left or the one on the right?

Answer on page 160.

Spinning Zig, Turning Zag

Sure, these shapes are locked into their positions on the page, but that doesn't stop them from at least appearing to move!

C
H
A
P
T
E
R

4

Chess Board

Which square is darker, **A** or **B**?

Answer on page 160.

Line Waves

Ride the waves as these opposing and multidimensional lines fold in on themselves.

Rainbow Bright

The colours in the top rainbow have completely faded. To brighten them back up, stare at the white dot in the bottom rainbow for 20 seconds, then shift your gaze back to the top rainbow. This illusion is based on colour adaptation and after-image effect.

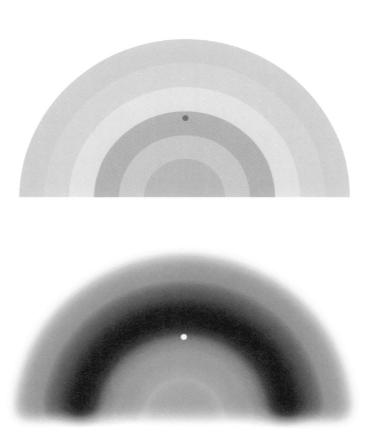

Anomalous Motion

If you let your eyes roam this image, you're likely to experience a warping effect. This is known as anomalous motion, a term used to define the appearance of motion in a static image. Colour contrasts and eye movement contribute to relative motion effects.

Shifting Lines

Notice how this image appears to have texture? It does not, though don't tell your eyes that. This illusion is caused by shifting some of the many lines out of their vertical placement.

Ferris Wheel

Take a trip on one of the world's most classic amusements: the Ferris wheel! And you don't have to leave your home. Just concentrate on this illusion from Herman Verwaal and watch the wheel spin.

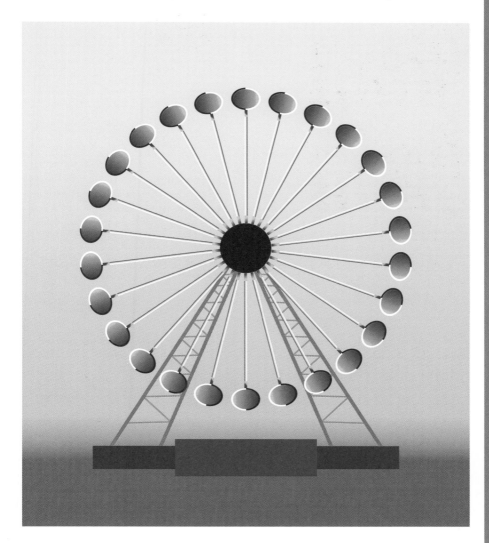

Answers

Tricky Terrace (page 7)
There are 2 ways to perceive this image: from below (figure **A**) or above (figure **B**). These kinds of illusions are known as bistable figures.

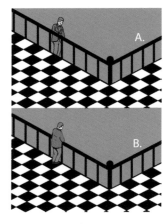

Santa Balance (page 10)
Though the scales are perfectly balanced, they seem to tilt to the left. This visual distortion is induced by the lines pointing towards the left side.

Scholars (page 15)
The man in the foreground is actually 15 per cent taller than the man in the background.

Stacked Perspective
(page 31)
The lines are perfectly straight; they only appear to run at angles due to the off-centre design of the black and white boxes.

Spiral Design (page 35)
The spiral in statue **A** is actually 2 spirals, while the spiral in **B** is a double spiral.

A. 2 spirals | B. 1 double spiral

Lingering Image (page 44)
The skull appears on the sheet of paper, only the blacks and whites are reversed.

Eyes Like a Hawk (page 46)
Look closely and you'll see the face of a rabbit concealed in the hawk's wing.

Look Closely (page 47)

90 Degrees (page 49)

There are 8 angles. Most people locate 6, though there are 2 deceptive angles hidden between the houses. Some of the angles may not look like right angles, but this is due to a trick of apparent perspective.

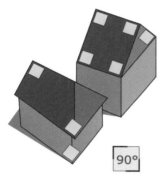

Ahoy, Matey! (page 50)

Flip the page—Blackbeard's face is concealed in the peacock's plumage.

Drawing the Line (page 51)

Fractured Letter (page 52)

All pieces are fractions of the letter **Z**.

Front/Back (page 53)

Read one way, the letters read "back"; reflected in a mirror, they read "front."

Author! Author! (page 55)

Don't Get Outfoxed
(page 58)

Here, Kitty... (page 59)
Turn the page upside down, and you'll find a butterfly in the cat's face.

Up in Smoke (page 61)

Read Between the Lines
(page 62)
The shapes reveal the following message: "Think the eyes have it."

Cheese Vision (page 63)
It would seem that **B** is the best fit, but the answer, when considering the exact angle and shape, is **A**.

Find the Lovers (page 65)

Ambigrams (page 66)
The words "sublime" and "apache" read exactly the same.

Missing Fs (page 67)
Most people count 6 **F**s, but there are actually 8! It's easy to glaze over the **F** in the preposition "of"—words such as "and," "from," and "of" are processed unconsciously by our minds.

Dog's Best Friend (page 68)
Below the dog's ear, you'll find the outline of a man's face.

Baaaffling Illusion (page 69)

Complete Drawing
(page 70)

Impatient Patients
(page 72)
The first face is hidden along the doctor's hairline; the second along his ear; the third on his right sleeve; the fourth along his jacket's tails; the fifth along his waistcoat.

Aloha! (page 73)
1. She has 2 left feet; 2. she has 6 fingers on her right hand (counting the concealed thumb).

Catching Some Zs (page 74)

Double Face (page 76)
There are 3 faces—2 looking directly at each other, and a third created by combining the 2 sides.

Hidden Alien (page 77)
The squares and rectangles form the shadows of the hidden letters **ET.**

Roll the Dice (page 78)
Even though the red dot on the farther die seems much larger, it is the exact same size as the red dot on the closer die. The illusion is a trick of perception.

Chopper Lines (page 79)
If you concentrate on the circles that surround the lines, the red one appears longer. But, if you concentrate on the helicopters instead, the blue one appears longer. The fact is that the blue is the longest of the pair.

Coy Fishing (page 80)
They are the same size. The bottom fish appears smaller because of its proximity to the glass edge; it appears tighter, and thus smaller.

Bed Lengths (page 81)

B.

Around in Circles (page 82)
They're all equal in length.

___ Is For... (page 83)
M

Circular Studies (page 84)
They are both the same size.

Parallelogram (page 86)
They are both the same length.

Pyramid Lines (page 88)
Yes, both lines are the same length.

Wider or Taller? (page 90)
Though it seems unlikely, the polo shirt is wider (**A** to **B**). The curved sleeves give the appearance of shorter length.

Copyrights (page 91)
They are all the same size. This illusion is known as an Ebbinghaus Illusion, which deals with relative size perception.

Split Line (page 92)
The top piece completes the line.

Landscape Length (page 94)
A to **B** is longer, though it seems that **A** to **C** would be the correct choice. This illusion is based on angled perspective.

Distorted Squares (page 95)
Though most people say **B**, the answer is **A**! In cases of perception distortion, the brain interprets regular lines or shapes in the foreground incorrectly; those lines and shapes get contrasted with other lines and shapes in the background, making them appear distorted.

Warping Effect? (page 96)
The outside lines make them appear to warp, but they remain level.

Strike! (page 99)
They are the same size. This is a variation of a Ponzo Illusion, which is based on how the brain perceives the size of an object based on its background.

Pick a Number (page 100)
9

R Shapes (page 101)
The green **R** and the red **R** are congruent.

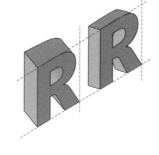

Long Lines (page 102)
Both are the same length. This is a variation of a Müller-Lyer Illusion, a size-consistency illusion.

Height Times Width (page 103)
Though it appears the **H** is wider, they are the same width.

Square Rings (page 104)
Both have the identical area of 12 square units each.

Bookends (page 107)
A connects to **C**.

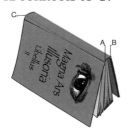

Connected Lines (page 109)
They are both the same length.

Pick a Number (page 110)
3

Line Difference (page 113)
They are the same length.

Square Holdings (page 114)
The top 2 are the same colour.

Comforting Illusion
(page 118)
Though it seems incredible, **A** and **C** are exactly alike. A colour always seems brighter when surrounded by dark colours, and vice versa.

Rotating Discs (page 122)
Neither—the motion is implied only by the rapid movement of your eyes and the colour contrasts between the shapes on their background.

The Blues (page 124)
Yes, they are the same shade of blue.

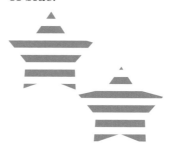

Straw Alignment (page 136)
It is not possible. Only diagonal lines of the same colour can be continuously linked together.

Crossroads (page 138)
The discs are all the same brightness. This illusion functions because of the brightness contrast in the background—that is why the discs appear to be different, even though they are not.

Star Contrast (page 141)

Yes, they are the same colour.

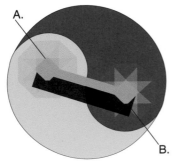

Centre Squares (page 146)

They are the same shade.

Chess Board (page 148)

They are actually the same colour. This is an effect of shadow and surrounding colours. **B** appears lighter, but only because the surrounding squares are darker, due to the shadow cast over them.

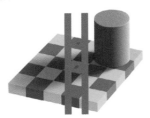